WITHDRAWN FROM DLR LIBRARIES STOCK

BAINTE DEN STOC

Local Environment

Sally Hewitt

W
FRANKLIN WATTS
LONDON·SYDNEY

This edition 2011
First published in 2008 by
Franklin Watts
338 Euston Road
London NW1 3BH

Franklin Watts Australia
Level 17/207 Kent Street
Sydney NSW 2000
Copyright © Franklin Watts 2008

Editor: Jeremy Smith
Art director: Jonathan Hair
Design: Jason Anscomb
All rights reserved.
A CIP catalogue record for this book
is available from the British Library.

Picture credits: Alamy: 6t, 7, 8, 10t, 13b, 18, 19b, 21cr,
22, 26-27. Dore Primary School: 11. istockphoto: 16t.
Kids for Tigers: a 23. Project Clean Sweep: 15. Ripple
Africa: 16b. Sherman Elementary School: 9.
Shutterstock: 5, 6b, 10b, 12, 13t,14, 18b, 19t, 21cl.
Southfields Primary School: 24. UNICEF: 17.

Every attempt has been made to clear copyright. Should
there be any inadvertent omission, please apply to the
publisher for rectification.

Dewey Classification: 941.085

ISBN: 978 1 4451 0600 7

Printed in China

Franklin Watts is a division of Hachette Children's Books,
an Hachette UK company.
www.hachette.co.uk

Contents

Local environment

Your local environment is your neighbourhood. Whether you live in a city, a village, by the seaside or in the countryside, you share your local environment with other people, plants and animals, so it's important to look after it.

Challenge!

Find out about the people, animals and plants that share your local environment.

- What can you do to be helpful and friendly to your neighbours?
- How can you help to keep your neighbourhood clean and safe?
- What could you do to look after local wild animals and plants?

This family live in a city. The neighbours in their street all help to make it a nice place to live.

Mr Tiddles

Mr Tiddles the pet cat was given a bell to wear on his collar. It warns local birds and small animals to run away when he goes hunting.

Pupils enjoy coming into a clean, bright school.

These children are enjoying the wildlife that lives in the trees and plants in their school grounds.

School building

The school building is part of your local environment. Keeping it clean, safe and attractive is good for everyone who works there. You can help to make sure it's good for the planet too (see page 9).

Keeping tidy

Litter makes a school look messy and uncared for inside. It can get into drains and harm wildlife outside.

Your school

Your school shares its neighbourhood with people, animals and plants, too. You can help to make sure your school is doing its best to care for the local environment.

Action!

- Encourage your school to use eco-friendly cleaning products. Powerful chemicals in some cleaning materials can harm the environment.
- Have a weekly competition for the cleanest, tidiest, brightest classroom.
- Make sure your school is litter free inside and outside.

The school playground

A school playground can be a safe place to play or relax in between lessons. It might have space to run and kick a ball, somewhere to sit in the shade, a climbing frame or even a garden.

There is somewhere for all the pupils in this playground. But is it a good place for plants and animals too?

Challenge!

Hold a playground survey. Find out:

- What kinds of different spaces there are in your playground.
- Are there places where plants and animals can grow and live?
- Could your playground be improved?
- What could you do to improve it?

Action!

Send out a questionnaire. Ask:

What do you like about the playground?

What don't you like?

Is it good for the pupils?

Is it good for plants and animals?

Is it good for the planet?

How would you like to see it improved?

Draw a plan of your "dream" playground.

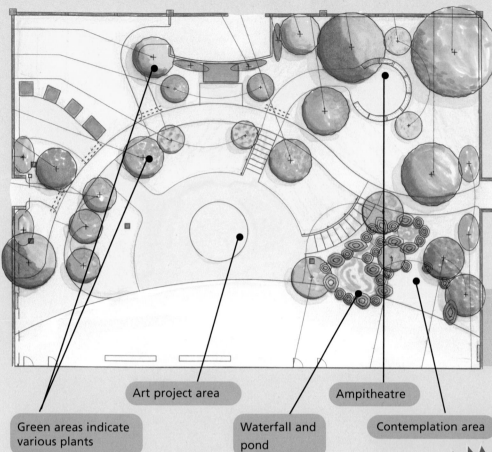

Everyone helped to plan a garden that had things to do and was good for the environment.

Art project area

Green areas indicate various plants

Waterfall and pond

Ampitheatre

Contemplation area

Case study – A green schoolyard

Some schools in San Francisco, USA, have been given the chance to change their school yards into "green schoolyards". There is space for the children to play, have outdoor lessons, grow plants and learn about wildlife and their local environment. Everything is built with materials that are friendly to the environment.

Sherman Elementary School, California, USA

At Sherman Elementary School, parents and children designed the schoolyard together (see top). Neighbours helped to build it. Everyone is involved in looking after it.

Asha Chan

"We love our new schoolyard – we get a chance to plant flowers and to watch them grow."

Asha Chan, Sherman Elementary School

Wildlife garden

You can grow plants and encourage animals to visit or make their homes wherever you live. Even if you don't have a garden you can grow plants in pots and window boxes which will attract insects and minibeasts, birds and small animals.

A super tidy garden like this one may look good, but it can be harmful to local wildlife.

Tidy gardens

There are no places for animals to hide and make their homes in a super tidy garden like the one shown on the left. Chemicals used in gardens to kill weeds and bugs kill other plants and animals too. Diagrams called food chains show how we all depend on other organisms in order to survive.

A Simple Food Chain

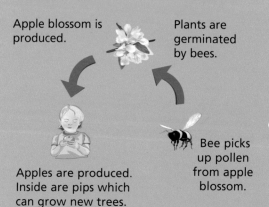

Apple blossom is produced.

Plants are germinated by bees.

Bee picks up pollen from apple blossom.

Apples are produced. Inside are pips which can grow new trees.

People, plants and animals depend on each other to survive. Without insects to carry pollen from flower to flower there would soon be no fruit, vegetables and seeds to eat.

Challenge!

Can you create a place for wildlife at school or where you live?

- Plant a window box with flowers that attract bees and butterflies.
- Make a pile of rocks where frogs or lizards can hide.
- Make a pile of leaves and twigs for minibeasts to hide.
- Ban harmful chemicals

Case study – Dore Primary School

Dore Primary School in Sheffield have created a wildlife garden by regenerating a disused area of the school grounds. They cleared it and planted a variety of plants, put up bird boxes and spruced up the bog garden.

Action!

Create a wildlife garden in your playground If your playground is very small, plant flowers and vegetables in containers and create spaces for animals in unused corners. Learn about plants and animals and their importance for the whole planet.

1

Alice says: "We had great fun identifying all the plants before we began work on our wildlife garden."

2

"This was an overgrown tip so we're doing something about it. After we had got to work and knuckled down we removed the cow parsley, nettles and thistles and now you can see the pond again."

3

"The storms brought down lots of branches. We are recycling them and using them as seats and path edges."

6

"It was hard work clearing the overgrown garden but it was great fun and looked great when we'd finished."

5

"To encourage birds to use the garden we put up nest boxes around the outside and two on trees in the garden."

4

"Digging out the paths was fantastic but a lot of hard work. We lined the paths and then put down bark chippings from the felled trees which were damaged in the storms."

11

Attracting wildlife

A wildlife-friendly garden doesn't just involve plants! You can attract wildlife at home or at school in many different ways. Make sure that you don't get unwanted visitors too!

A bird bath gives birds somewhere to have a wash and a drink.

Attract birds

A bird bath gives birds somewhere to have a wash and a drink. It can just be an old dish or plastic container. Put up feeders in a place that only birds can reach. If they are too low to the ground, you may find other animals such as squirrels will help themselves to food put out for the birds!

Endangered animals

In an environment with towns and cities, roads and modern farms, animals find it difficult to find places to make their homes. Owls, for example, used to nest in old fashioned farm buildings. Now they are becoming endangered. Nesting boxes provide a welcome home. Place them where cats and other hunters cannot reach, however.

An owl box placed high in a tree could encourage owls to nest there.

Goldfish and ducks make a splash of colour in ponds. They eat pond insects and their eggs.

Action!

Build a pond in your own back garden or at school to attract frogs and toads and pond insects.

- Dig a hole that is deep in the middle and shallow at the edges.
- Line the hole with some old carpet.
- Line the carpet with strong, waterproof pond liner.
- Hold down the edges of the pond liner with big stones.
- Fill the pond with rainwater.
- Plant some water plants.

Ponds

Ponds attract all kinds of wildlife. Fish swim underwater and frogs, toads and newts live in the water. Around the edges of the pond, insects hover and skim across the water and water birds search for food.

Challenge!

- Find out which animals and birds share your local environment.
- Decide which ones you would like to attract.
- Find the best ways to attract birds, small mammals, frogs, toads and reptiles.

 Ponds can be dangerous. Only visit a pond with an adult and make sure there is a fence around a school pond.

Sally Steve Jemma

A pond can be an outdoor classroom. These children are learning about the frog that has made its home in the school pond!

Litter

Litter is sometimes called "waste in the wrong place". Chewing gum on the pavement, an old sofa dumped by the side of the road, a plastic bag floating in the sea are all examples of litter. Litter is ugly and dirty and it can be dangerous, too.

Challenge!

Don't be a litterbug!

- Never drop litter.
- When you are out, always put your litter in the bin.
- Even better, take your litter home with you and get rid of it responsibly.
- Recycle litter whenever you can.
- Try and reduce the litter you make.

Dumping large amounts of litter in the wrong place is called "fly tipping". It is illegal in many countries. It should be taken to a tip to be buried or recycled.

Dangerous litter

If litter is washed down the drain it can pollute the water system. It can also block the drains and cause floods! Wind and rain carry litter into streams and rivers and then out to sea where it can strangle or choke animals, sea birds and fish. Broken glass causes cuts and accidents Food left to rot soon starts to smell and attract flies and rats which spread germs. Piles of litter can even cause fire in buildings and forests.

Piles of litter burn easily and can easily start forest fires. These devastate the animal community that lives within them.

Volunteering

Volunteers all over the world give up their spare time to clean up their local environment to make it a safer, healthier place for people and animals to live.

Case study – Project Clean Sweep

Clean the Bay is an organisation working to clear litter from Narragansett Bay and the Rhode Island shoreline on the east coast of America. It was started by two sailors worried about the amount of rubbish that was growing year by year. Clean Sweep is one of Clean the Bay's biggest projects. During Clean Sweep 1, 450 volunteers of all ages picked up small pieces of litter along the shoreline.

"Project Clean Sweep is a wonderful example of how individual citizens can accomplish great things."

Donald L. Carcieri, Governor of Rhode Island

Project Clean Sweep

1 Small pieces of plastic are washed ashore. If they are not picked up, animals could eat them and choke or become poisoned.

2 Parents and children picked up litter together on a family day out.

4 Volunteers put on strong gloves to collect small pieces of litter in strong paper bags that are biodegradable.

3 Bulldozers and lifting gear were used to clear big pieces of litter.

Trees

Trees play an important part in keeping the planet clean and healthy. A gas in the air called carbon dioxide is helping to cause climate change. Trees take in carbon dioxide and give out oxygen – the gas that we need to breathe.

All over the world, rainforests are being cut down for farming and timber. Where this happens, plants and animals lose their home and start to die out. Fewer trees means more carbon dioxide in the air.

These beautiful old trees provide welcome shelter for this school in Kenya, Africa.

Wonderful trees

Trees are wonderful! they help to keep the air clean. Woods and forests are home for other plants and animals.

Trees give us shade and shelter from the sun and rain, and building materials for our homes. Trees are beautiful. Can you imagine a world without trees?

Sustainable wood

Once cut down, rainforest trees take hundreds of years to grow again, and sometimes a forest is never re-grown. Wood that comes from forests of fast growing trees such as pine which are replanted when cut down is called "sustainable".

Case study –
Plant for the Planet

Under the Plant for the Planet: Billion Tree Campaign, people, communities, organisations, business and industry, and governments are being encouraged to plant trees and enter their tree planting pledges on this web site. The objective is to plant at least one billion trees worldwide every year. Children at the first Africa Region Children's Conference planted 5,000 trees as a contribution to the Billion Tree Campaign in Yaoundé, the capital city of Cameroon.

A boy ready to plant a tree in Cameron.

Challenge!

Find out what is made of wood at home and at school, for example, building materials, furniture, climbing frames or paper.

When your family or school buy things made from wood, check to see if the wood is from a sustainable forest.

➡ Action!

Plant a tree!

- Choose a tree seedling that is native to where you live.
- Find a suitable place to plant it with plenty of room for the full grown tree.
- Dig a hole deep and wide enough for the roots.
- Plant seedling and press earth round it gently and firmly.
- Feed and water it.

Your local park

A park that is clean and free of litter and full of plants and flowers can be enjoyed by everyone. It is a great place for holding a sports day a picnic or a fair where the whole community can get together and have a good time.

Children play together in their local park.

Dog mess

Dog mess is dirty, smelly and full of germs. If dog mess is left lying around on the grass, germs can be spread and people can become ill. Picking it up helps to keep the park a safer, cleaner place. Paper or cardboard are better for the job than plastic bags. They degrade much faster and are better for the environment.

Challenge!

Take a walk in the park.

• Are there litter bins?

• Are there poop-a-scoop bins?

• Do people use the bins?

• Is the playground safe and well looked after?

• Are there benches to sit on?

• Are the trees and flowers well cared for?

• Is it a nice place to play, have a picnic or go for a walk?

Graffiti spoils the environment for other people.

Graffiti

Graffiti shows disrespect for whatever it is sprayed on. If there is graffiti in the park, you know some visitors aren't caring for it properly. Graffiti should be reported to your local council.

A tidy park is a great place for sports such as football.

Enjoy your park

Everyone can enjoy a park that is free of dog mess, litter and graffiti and is full of plants and flowers. Sports teams can play on the grass, children can play in the playground and families can go for a walk safely.

 Action!

Get involved with your local park.

• Some parks are in danger of being closed. Is yours? Fight to keep it open if so. Find out how you or your school could help to improve your park.

• Help to make it a place for people to enjoy themselves and for wild animals to make their home.

Pollution

The air you breathe, the soil your fruit and vegetables grow in and the water you drink and wash with are all part of your local environment. All are in danger of being polluted but there are things you can do to help to keep them clean.

If air, water and soil are clean, it will help the people, animals and plants that depend on them for life to be healthy.

Pollution such as exhaust fumes is bad for both plants and people.

Polluted air

Chemicals in cleaning sprays, traffic exhaust, smoke from factory chimneys and houses and cigarette smoke all pollute the air and are bad for us to breathe. Everyone can help to keep the air cleaner by using natural and eco-friendly cleaners, by walking, cycling or taking the bus or train, by saving electricity at home and at school and by not smoking.

Challenge!

Go clean and green at home and school.

You can clean yourself, your home and your school with eco-friendly products that won't pollute your local environment.

Water

Chemicals from cleaning products are washed down the drain. Fertilisers and weed killers in the soil drain into the water system. All these polluting chemicals have to be cleaned in water treatment plants.

Soil

Chemical fertilisers, weed and pest killers get into the soil and into the plants we eat. They harm animals that live in the soil and insects that visit the plants. Organic compost enriches the soil and some plants, such as marigolds, dill and nasturtium, help to keep pests away naturally.

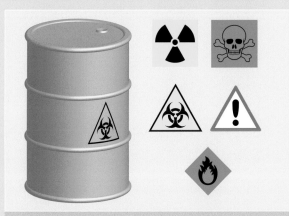

Get to know the signs that let you know which chemicals are dangerous.

Toxic waste

When you change to eco-friendly products, don't pour the old products down the drain or just throw them away. They are toxic! Find out how to dispose of them responsibly.

Put plants around your home and school They take in gas called carbon dioxide and other pollutants in the air and give out oxygen for you to breathe.

 **Action!**

Natural cleaners

Encourage your parents and your school to use them as cheap, alternative cleaners.

- Baking soda cleans and gets rid of smells.
- Washing soda dissolves grease.
- White vinegar and lemon juice clean surfaces.
- Vegetable oil is a polish.

 Warning!

Even natural products are chemicals. Don't touch anything without adult supervision.

Wear gloves.

Remember! Test natural cleaners on a small area first.

Your community

Your school is part of a community of all the people who live and work the area. Schools can get involved in local projects and work with people in their community to make it a cleaner, healthier place for everyone to live in.

You can joined a local group of volunteers and help to reclaim a local natural area such as a stream, meadow or woodland.

Protecting your environment

The way people live means that the environment around us is in constant threat from the activities of people. Builders and developers are always looking for places to build new houses, while councils look to find space to construct new roads. Find out what the issues are and decide whether you think your local environment is in danger. If you think it is, join a campaign to stop the danger. Contact your councillor or MP. Sign a petition.

Challenge!

Get involved with a community project

- Find out about an environmental issue that affects your community.
- Work on it with other members of your community.
- Find out if there is an organisation that will fund you or give you a grant.

Case study - Kids for Tigers

Tigers are in danger. Even though they are protected, poachers shoot them for their beautiful coats, their teeth and bones. Their natural habitat is also under threat. Tigers need space to roam around and hunt for food. Their natural home is in the vast forests of India, but the forests are getting smaller and smaller and, tigers are finding it harder to find enough food to survive.

Saving the forests is an important part of the Kids for Tigers campaign. Kids for Tigers teaches and encourages Indian school children to get involved in saving wild tigers and their habitats.

Ananya, Devayani and Devika Chandra of The Shri Ram School.

"Help! The tigers are dying and all we are doing is watch them die. If we as little children know this, how come adults don't know?"

Kids for Tigers campaign.

1 Walking the Palm Beach nature trail in India, children experienced the amazing scenery, plants and animals of a tiger's home.

2 School children worked together on a long roll of material called a "scroll" explaining the plight of the Indian tiger.

3 School children marched at a Save the Tiger rally in Bangalore.

Action!

Find out which organisations might help you, for example:

- A local wildlife organisation
- Woodland or forest organisation
- Zoo
- Botanical garden
- Charity
- Local authority
- Other schools
- Local businesses

Making links

Schools make links with each other across the world to support and learn from each other. They find out about each other's local environments, how they affect it and how it affects them.

Clean water

Lack of water affects plants, animals and people. Nyogbare Primary in Ghana is in a dry area. It had no access to clean water. Pupils in the UK who are used to having lots of clean running water learnt to appreciate how important clean water supply is. Both schools worked together to make a difference and get something done.

"We are grateful for the concern Southfields have for our brothers and sisters in Nyogbare. The construction of the bore hole is complete and the children, teachers and communities close to the school are enjoying the water. We are about to start the safe hygiene training in the school."

Gani Tijani, Director of Rural Aid in the Upper East Region of Ghana.

Southfields Primary School in Coventry linked with Nyogbare Primary in Ghana. They helped to pay for a water pump for the children to use (above).

Adopt a habitat
Find out all you can about it
- what animals and plants live there
- what is threatening the habitat you have chosen?
- what you can do to help?
- join an organisation that will help you.

Environments under threat

Many factors threaten local environments such as forests, wetlands, coastlines, coral reefs. It's important for people to find ways of living and working in harmony with the environment. Here is a list of the ways in which humans can threaten the environment around them.

Challenge!

Twin or link with a school in another part of the world.
Learn about each other's daily lives and local environment.

Find out how you can work together to improve the lives of the pupils, animals and plants in the local environment.

People
There are so many of us that we are taking up more and more space. We must remember that we share our world with plants and animals.

Farming
Huge areas of land are cleared to grow crops for food and materials such as wood and cotton.

Industry
We are using up natural resources such as coal, gas, oil and metal. Pollution from factories, homes and transport can threaten local environments.

Tourism
People want to travel to beautiful places but tourists can be responsible for causing damage. Responsible tourists can help to save the places they visit.

Coral reefs are under threat from pollution, and tourism can also damage the delicate coral.

Spread the word

You can form a Green Team in your school with your friends to help the environment. Share what you have learned with the whole school, parents and friends. Make sure everyone knows what you are doing.

Challenge!

Make a list of ways you can pass on information.
Make a plan and give yourselves a time limit to get everything done.

Make a plan of ways you can make a difference and share it with friends.

Kim

Paul

Rasha

Dijal

Lucy

Enfield Primary School have set up a Green Team. These members share information with the whole school at assembly.

Local news
Your local newspaper, radio or TV station will be interested in local issues and what local schools are doing. Invite them to your special events or send out press releases with photographs.

Green team members post the latest eco-news on the school website.

Posters

Design posters about your local environment. Put them up in school and get permission to put them up in local shops and libraries. If there is a local event or meeting, put up posters and make sure everyone knows about it.

School website

Have you got a school website? If so, set up a Green Team news page. Keep it up-to-date with information and news about your green projects. Include ideas of how everyone can join in.

Ask your school if you can put up posters to support what you are doing.

Action!

- Hold a school assembly.
- Write and perform a play.
- Have a poster campaign.
- Write newsletters and send them out.
- Post news and information on the school website.
- Send press releases to your local newspaper, radio or TV station.

Glossary

Audit
An audit is a check. An audit to find out if your playground is eco-friendly could check if it is a good place for children, animals and plants to live, and if the soil and air around it are clean.

Campaign
A campaign is action taken to get something done.

Community
A community is all the people who live and work in a neighbourhood. Plants and animals are part of the community too.

Eco-friendly
Eco-friendly means not being harmful to the environment or to the plants and animals that live in it.

Environment
The environment is everything around you. You might live in a built-up environment such as a city or in a natural environment such as the countryside.

Endangered
Endangered means at risk. Endangered animals are at risk of dying out and becoming extinct.

Grant
A grant is money given to help with a project. A grant is usually given by an organisation or the government.

Green team
A school green team is a group of children and staff who work together to protect the planet and the environment.

Organic
Natural, not man-made. Organic farming uses as few chemicals and artificial pesticides as possible, and farmers rear animals without the routine use of drugs.

Organisation
An organisation is group of people running a business or a charity.

Sustainable
If something is sustainable, it can be kept going. Using natural resources such as wood or oil in a sustainable way means using it in a way that doesn't use it all up or destroy part of the natural environment.

Volunteer
A volunteer is somebody who works without being paid.

Weblinks

www.lcd.org.uk
Link Community Development works to improve education for children and to link schools all over the world.

www.unep.org
The United Nations Environment Programme
Its aim is to give leadership and encourage people to work as partners in caring for the environment.

www.wwf.org/
The World Wildlife Fund is an organisation that protects animals in their natural habitats all over the world.

http://gowild.wwf.org.uk/gowild
The World Wildlife Fund for kids.

www.unep.org/billiontreecampaign/
The United Nations Environment Programme (UNEP) has launched a major worldwide tree planting campaign.

www.woodland-trust.org.uk/
Woodland Trust is a conservation charity dedicated to the protection of native woodland heritage in the UK.

www.kidsfortigers.org/
Kids take action to help save tigers in India.

Note to parents and teachers:

Every effort has been made by the Publishers to ensure that these websites are suitable for children, that they are of the highest educational value, and that they contain no inappropriate or offensive material. However, because of the nature of the Internet, it is impossible to guarantee that the contents of these sites will not be altered. We strongly advise that Internet access is supervised by a responsible adult.

Index